DATE DUE

Pebble® Plus

Exploring the Galaxy

Venus

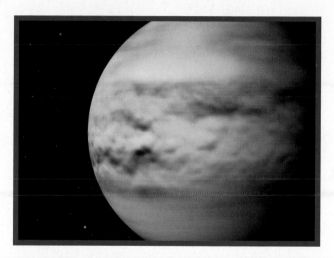

by Thomas K. Adamson

Consulting Editor: Gail Saunders-Smith, PhD

Consultant: James Gerard
Aerospace Education Specialist, NASA
Kennedy Space Center, Florida

Capstone press®

Mankato, Minnesota

Revised and Updated

Pebble Plus is published by Capstone Press,
151 Good Counsel Drive, P.O. Box 669, Mankato, Minnesota 56002.
www.capstonepress.com

1 2 3 4 5 6 12 11 10 09 08 07

Library of Congress Cataloging-in-Publication Data
Adamson, Thomas K., 1970–
    Venus / by Thomas K. Adamson.—Rev. and updated.
    p. cm.—(Pebble plus. Exploring the galaxy)
    Includes bibliographical references and index.
    ISBN-13: 978-1-4296-0739-1 (hardcover)
    ISBN-10: 1-4296-0739-4 (hardcover)
    1. Venus (Planet)—Juvenile literature. I. Title. II. Series.
QB621.A33 2008
523.42—dc22
                                                            2007004457

Summary: Simple text and photographs describe the planet Venus.

Editorial Credits
Mari C. Schuh, editor; Kia Adams, designer; Alta Schaffer, photo researcher

Photo Credits
Digital Vision, cover, 5 (Venus), 7, 9 (Venus), 15
NASA, 17; JPL, 5 (Jupiter); JPL/Caltech, 5 (Uranus)
PhotoDisc Inc., 4 (Neptune), 5 (Mars, Mercury, Earth, Sun, Saturn), 9 (Earth), 13; Stock Trek, 11; PhotoDisc Imaging, 1, 19
Photo Researchers, Inc./Jerry Schad, 21

Note to Parents and Teachers

The Exploring the Galaxy set supports national science standards related to earth science. This book describes and illustrates the planet Venus. The photographs support early readers in understanding the text. The repetition of words and phrases helps early readers learn new words. This book also introduces early readers to subject-specific vocabulary words, which are defined in the Glossary section. Early readers may need assistance to read some words and to use the Table of Contents, Glossary, Read More, Internet Sites, and Index sections of the book.

Table of Contents

Venus

Venus is the second planet
from the Sun.
Venus and the other planets
move around the Sun.

The Solar System

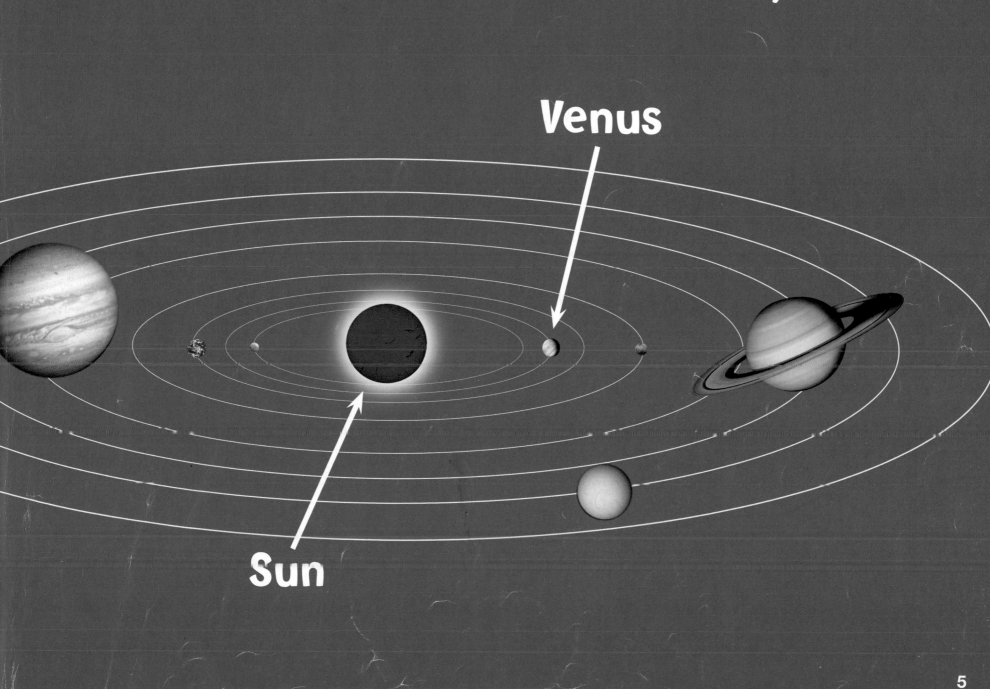

Venus

Sun

Venus is the third brightest
object in the sky.
Only the Sun and
Earth's moon are brighter
than Venus.

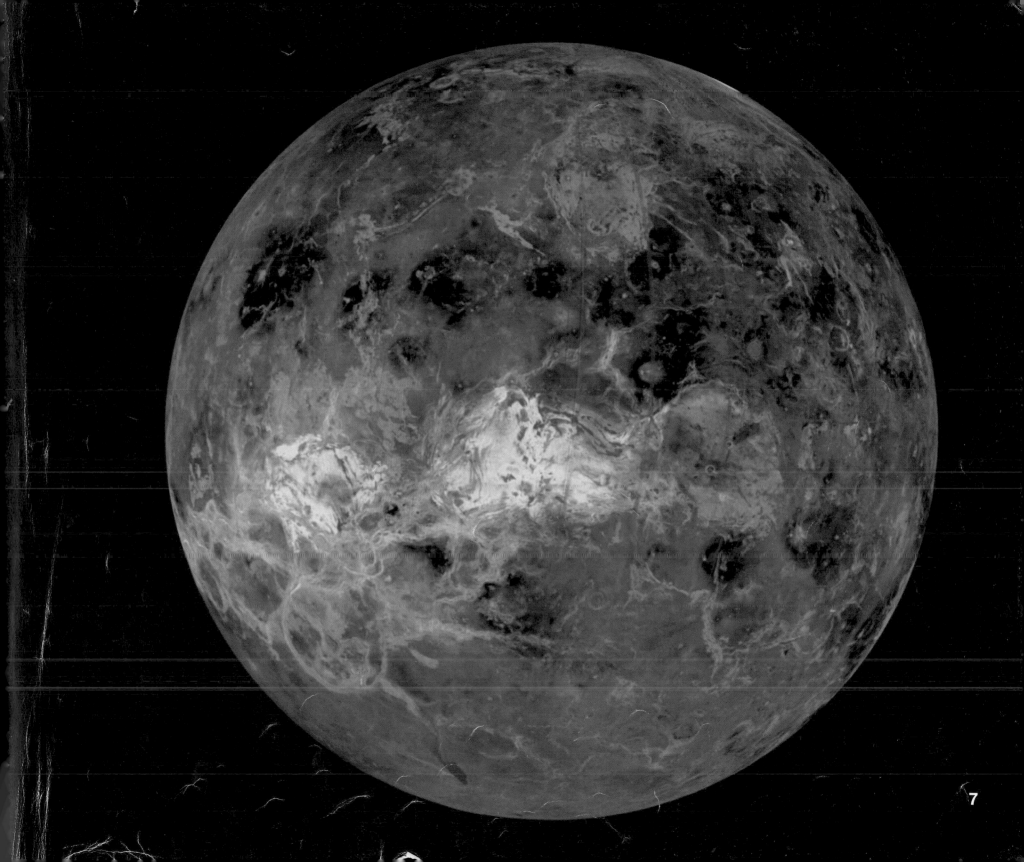

Size of Venus

Venus is almost

the same size as Earth.

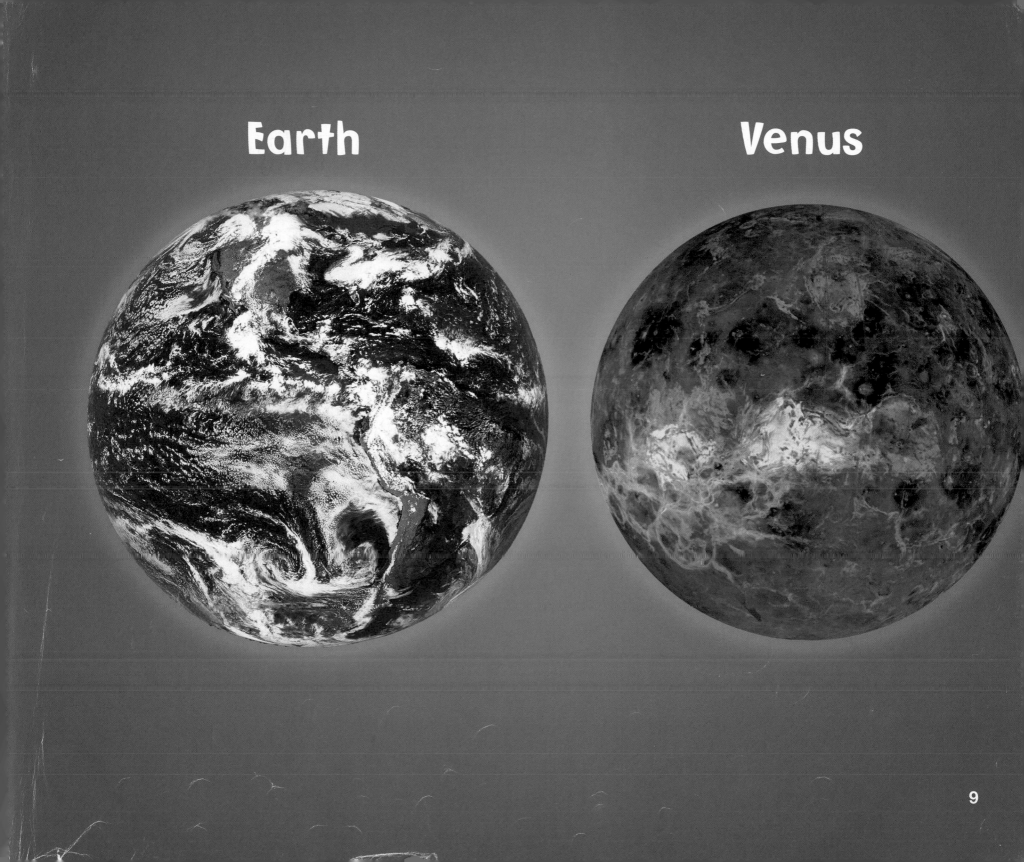

Earth

Venus

Air and Land

Venus is the hottest planet.

The surface of Venus

is hotter than an oven.

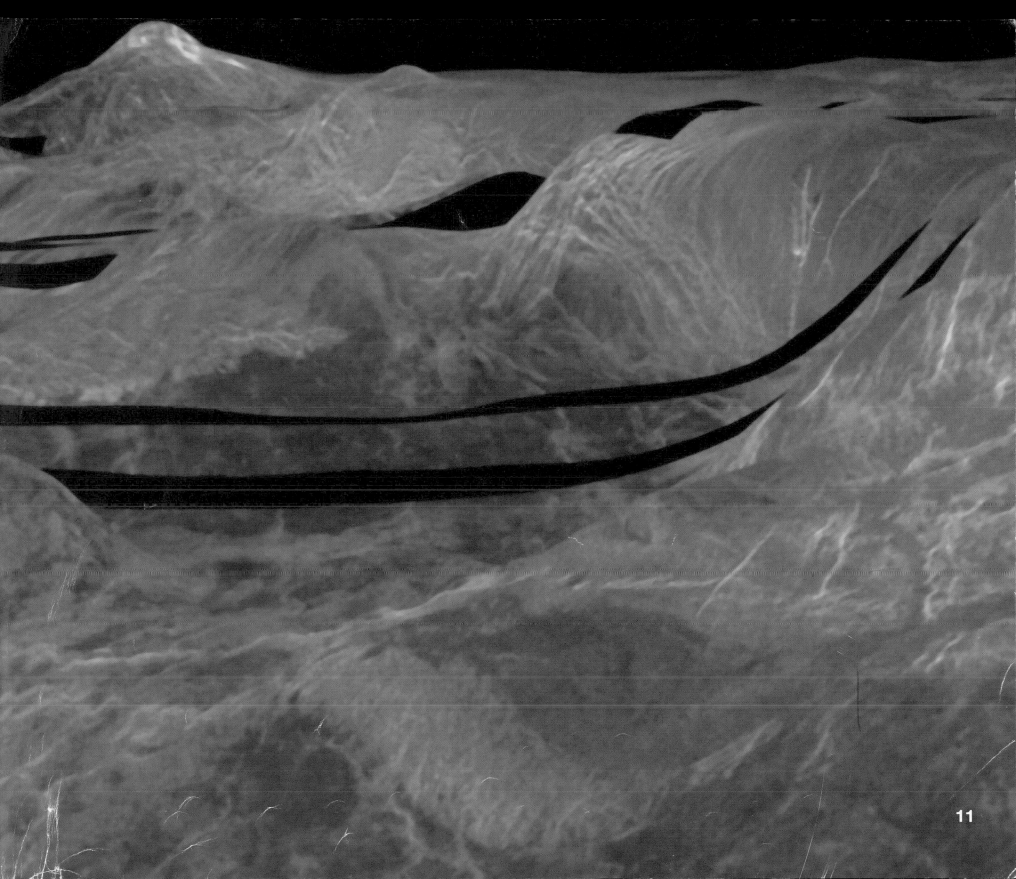

11

Venus has hundreds
of volcanoes.
Thousands of craters
cover Venus.

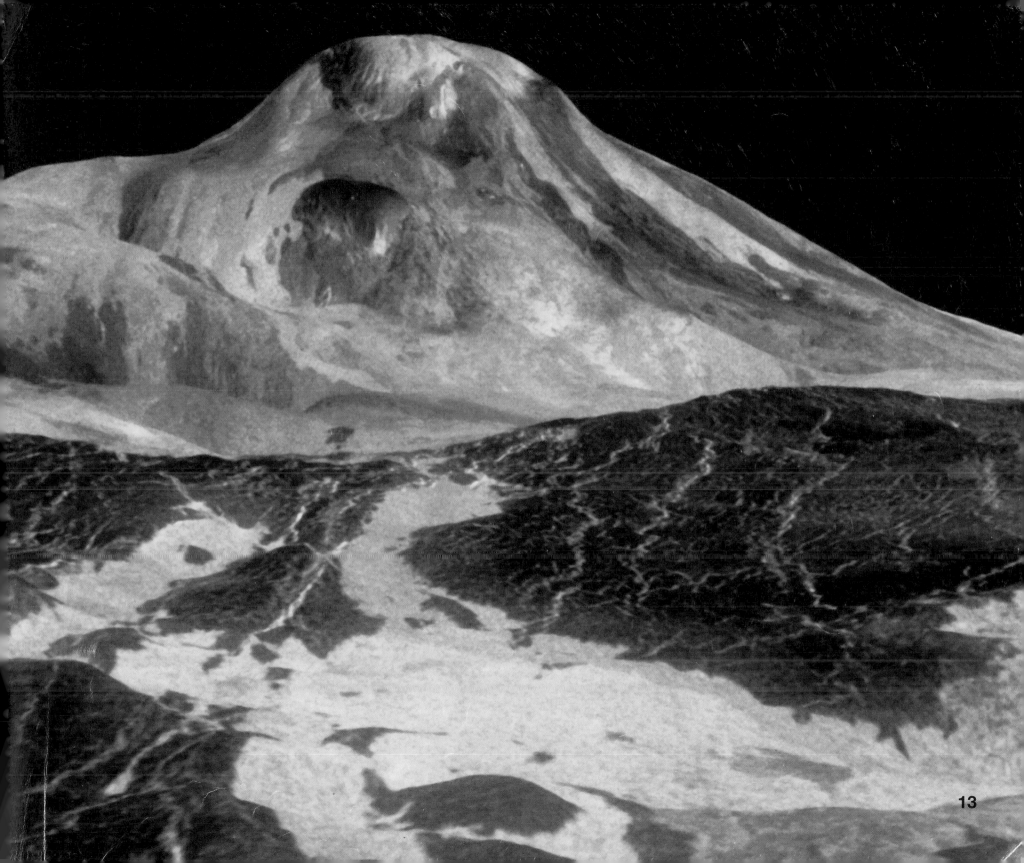

Thick clouds made
of acid cover Venus.

The clouds on Venus trap

the Sun's heat.

The clouds make

the air heavy.

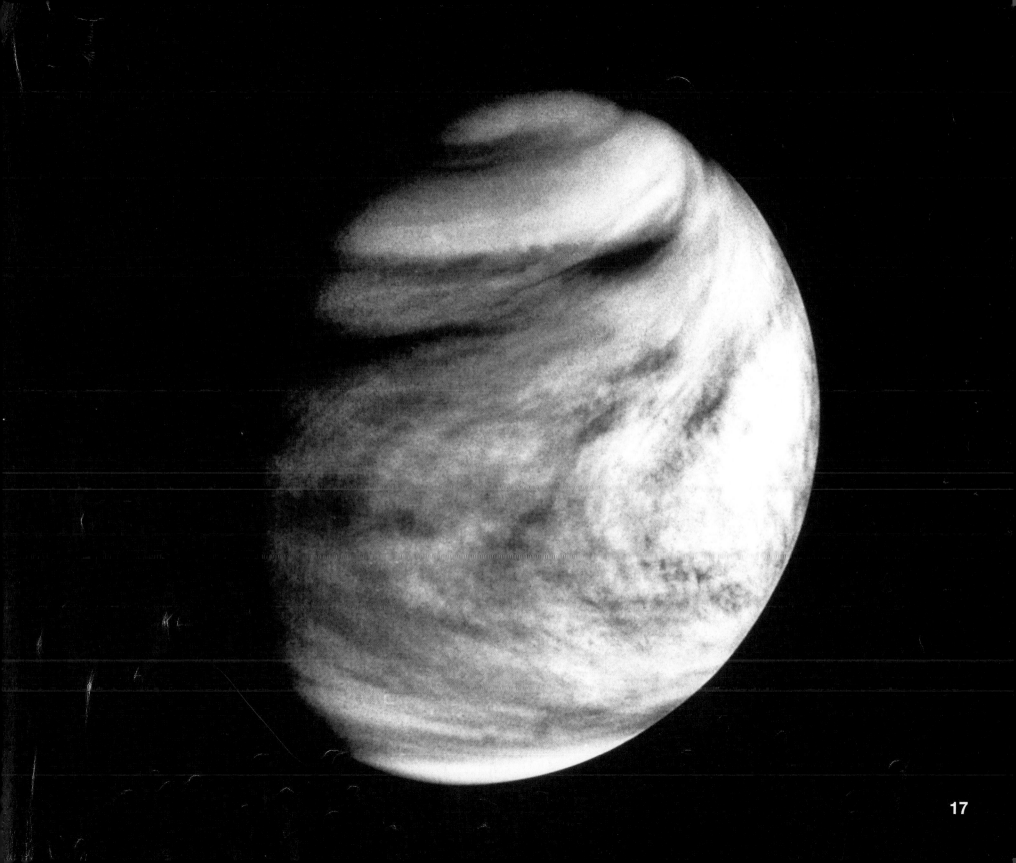

People and Venus

People cannot live on Venus.

The heat would cook them.

The heavy air would

crush them.

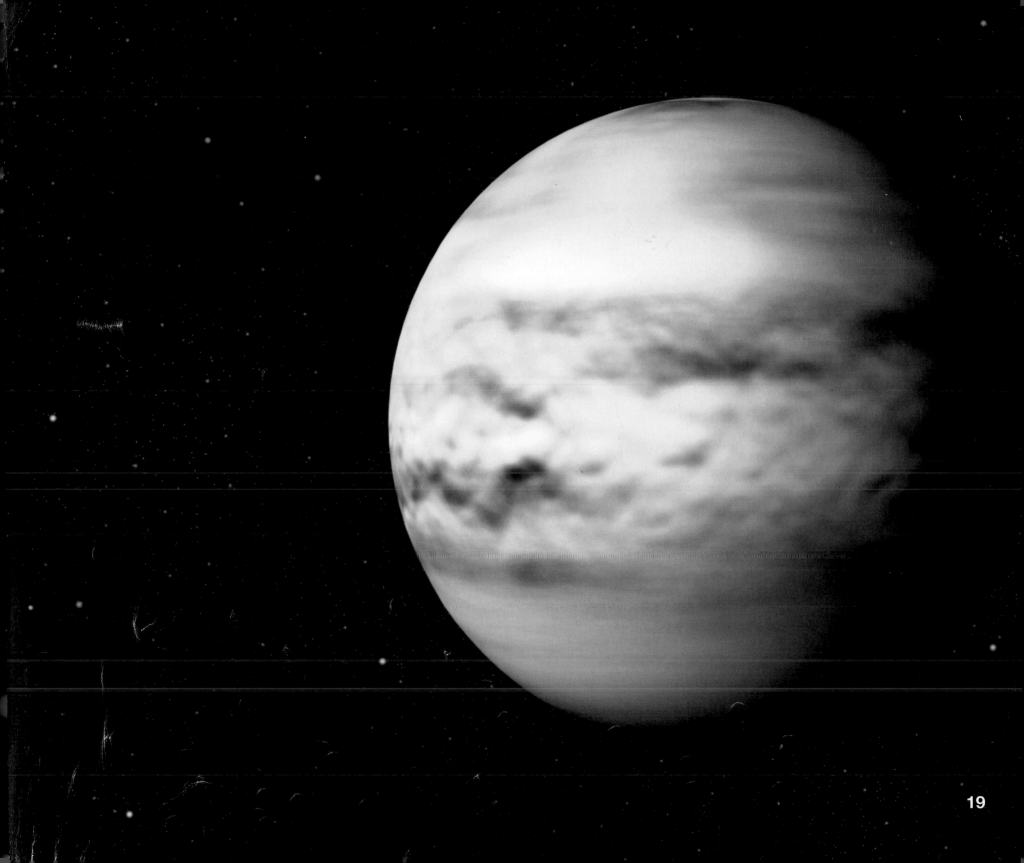

People can sometimes
see Venus from Earth.
Venus looks like
a bright star.

Glossary

acid—a substance that can harm people

crater—a large hole in the ground; many craters on planets are caused by falling pieces of rock.

oven—an enclosed space, like a stove, where people bake or roast food

planet—a large object that moves around the Sun; Venus is closer to the Sun than Earth is; there are eight planets in the solar system.

Sun—the star that the planets move around; the Sun provides light and heat for the planets.

volcano—a mountain with vents; melted rock oozes out of the vents; volcanoes on Venus are no longer active.

Read More

Olien, Rebecca. *Exploring the Planets in Our Solar System.* Objects in the Sky. New York: PowerKids Press, 2007.

Richardson, Adele. *Venus.* First Facts: The Solar System. Mankato, Minn.: Capstone Press, 2008.

Wimmer, Teresa. *Venus.* My First Look at Planets. Mankato, Minn.: Creative Education, 2007.

Internet Sites

FactHound offers a safe, fun way to find Internet sites related to this book. All of the sites on FactHound have been researched by our staff.

Here's how:

1. Visit *www.facthound.com*

2. Choose your grade level.

3. Type in this book ID **1429607394** for age-appropriate sites. You may also browse subjects by clicking on letters, or by clicking on pictures and words.

4. Click on the **Fetch It** button.

FactHound will fetch the best sites for you!

Index

Word Count: 118
Grade: 1
Early-Intervention Level: 14